"PERCY"

GROWING UP

BY

HELEN POWELL WHITE

Helen Powell White

Published
By
Ash Grove Publishing
Diamond, Ohio 44412

Library of Congress
Cataloging-in-Publication Data

Library of Congress Control Number: 2010901889

ISBN-13: 9780615351049

ISBN-10: 0615351042

Copyright © 2010 by Helen Powell White

First Edition - 2010

Printed in the United States of America
All Rights Reserved

*Dedicated To The Beloved Dogs Who Have Shared Our Lives
With Love*

*Sweet tears still hide whenever I speak your name. Your, beautiful
Watchful eyes linger on my mind and my heart shall never let you go.*

THE TALE

OF

A

TEDDY ROOSEVELT TERRIER

WELCOME TO OUR WORLD

Once inside The Enchanted Cottage, the tale of "Percy", The Perfect Puppy, continued. He lived in a special home. It was a place where love could be felt, that was not forced or for selfish reasons. It was a place where imperfections were not judged, where one could be at ease. It was a place where one felt safe and secure. Unexpected and sometimes delightful things occurred there. Almost always, happiness covered this world and when sadness moved in, comfort and love came to soothe it away. It was more than the walls and the yard. It was more than the flowers and the trees.

It was more than the people and the pets therein. It was a feeling of magical warmth, a feeling reflected in the lives of those who lived there and came to visit.

There was a unique charm in this quaint cottage. Although it was located in America's heartland, it reminded one of a home in England, in a time gone by. An antique piano and other old-fashioned furnishings graced the rooms. The old wood burning cook-stove was used at times for delicious, unforgettable meals.

A country garden of flowers and evergreens bordered the yard. The home's many windows brought beautiful views inside. In this peaceful setting, surrounded by nature, visitors were always welcome.

Beyond the cottage, on the property, was the trail 'Patty-Hands Path' that led through the woods to the meadow. Then across the road was their beautiful, 'Arthur Park'. Perhaps it was heaven on earth.

"Yes Ashley, The Enchanted Cottage was real."

When evening arrived, the moon and stars spread a soft, dim light and the trees cast expressive shadows across the grass. The cottage looked majestic, as it seemed to glow in the dark. Everything was now sheltered from the harshness of the day.

The night was beautiful.

Inside, the cottage was silent.
It was very, very silent.

All was well.

Upstairs, in a cozy bedroom, on the big bed, was a reflection of something white. Approaching closer, one could see in the dark, the figure of a sleeping dog. It was Percy. Curled up on his pillow, with his short little legs folded sweetly together, his ears arched upward in true terrier style, and his eyes closed, Percy was fast asleep. There was something very tender in this moment. Percy was just that precious.

PERCY

He was now full grown.

Gone were the days when he had to sleep in a cage or be watched so he did not get into trouble. He had learned not to take slippers and socks and run around the house, gleefully showing them off.

He was a good dog all the time, and was allowed the complete run of the house. So at night, Percy's pleasure was to sleep on the big bed upstairs, next to his master (who was the little lady).

This was where you would find him.

As the restful night gave way to morning, Percy was up and about, walking around on top of the bed, stirring up the covers. He was better than an alarm clock. The little lady was very happy to see him.

But sadly, "Ginger", the elegant Rottweiler was not there to wash Percy's face. Her gentle presence was gone, for she had left for puppy heaven.

Ginger had lived a very long time and had given so much pleasure to many people. When she died, both Percy and the furry dog Winston were at her burial. Ginger was laid to rest in a quiet, secluded garden at The Enchanted Cottage.

Watching and sniffing, the dogs seemed to understand what had happened.

The Memory Garden

The family did not wish to dwell continually on the sadness of loosing Ginger, but rather chose to remember all the good times and happy memories they had of her.

Ginger lived on in their hearts.

The trio, Percy, Ginger and Winston
She had the best smile!

Waiting for Percy downstairs was his buddy Winston. After their trip to the yard, and breakfast, there was a good game of tug and chase in the living room.

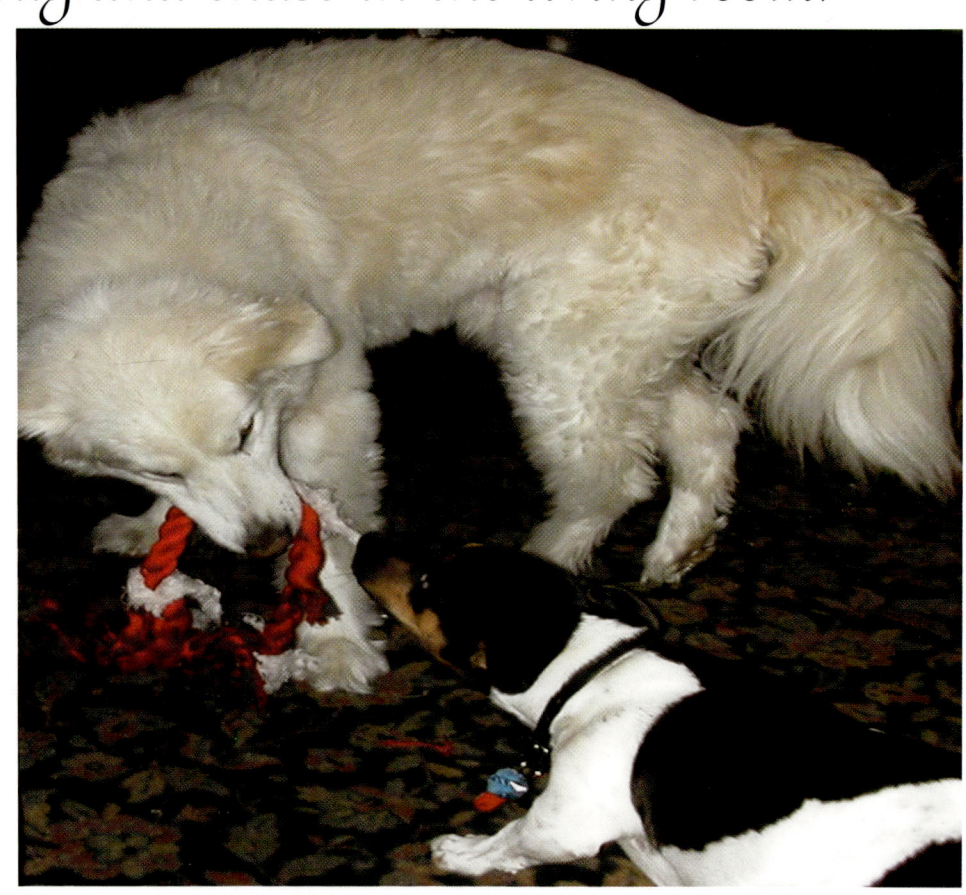

Who was stronger?

At times it got rather wild, as each dog knew exactly how to outsmart the other. But they played fairly.

Snatching was Winston's best game, while dodging and running came easily to Percy. They took turns letting each other have his way. Percy ran with the rope and circled Winston, teasing him. Percy then gave it up easily, so Winston could grab it and wave it around.

It was pleasing to see how kind the two dogs were to each other. There was no meanness, just pure fun. And when the game was over, the two rested side by side. They showed the simple truth, that:

To have a friend,
YOU MUST BE A FRIEND.

Percy and Winston looked out for one another. They looked forward to being together and doing things together.

Each was a friend to the other.

Winston On The Look Out

Located near the cottage was a small apple orchard. In the fall, these trees provided abundant food for the wildlife. The deer knew about the apples and they liked to come for a visit.

Regularly, Winston watched for the deer. If he spied them, he would sound the alarm. With one sharp bark, both Percy and he would be at the window, telling them, to "GET OUT OF OUR YARD".

For two sweet dogs, they did not sound very nice. And the closer the deer approached, the louder they barked: WOOF WOOF **WOOF! WOOF! WOOF!** The sound was awful! The only way to get the dogs to quit was to close the curtains. When the dogs could not see the deer, they stopped their barking. The deer could then pass through the yard peacefully.

    Percy and Winston did not like the deer and wanted to chase them away. The little lady knew this would not happen. Much to the dog's dismay, Percy and Winston were never allowed to go out and run them off, on an unfriendly, ill advised, 'Deer Patrol'.

    She kept them out of trouble.

Her short poem describes the deer's visit:

Gentle creatures with stately grace
Enter the yard for apples to taste
They hesitate, with each cautious step
Checking to see if the dogs are kept
Safe inside, where their barks are heard
Far from meeting their teeth or fur
Onward they travel with nary a sound
At times only hoof prints are there to be found

Yet stopping a moment for an apple or two
Then back to the woods to stay out of view

But we know they are watching

And will visit at night

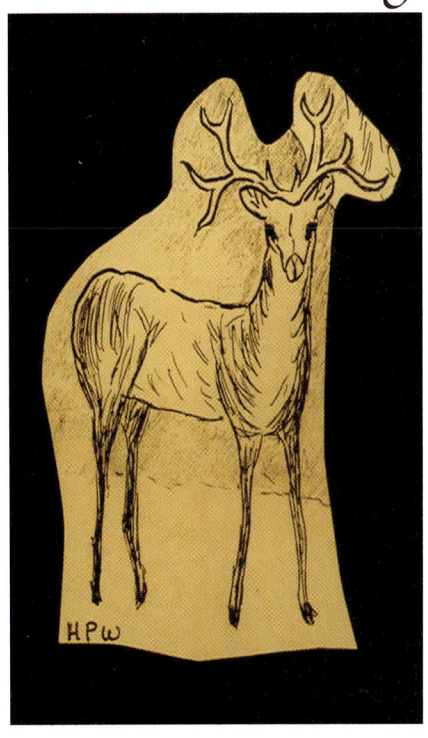

By the light of the moon
They're a beautiful sight.

Do you remember "Sardi" the donkey?

Our Gentle Friend

As the weather turned colder, he spent most of the days in his hotel. Daily Percy and the little lady would visit, taking Sardi his food, water and treats. As they walked toward ~ Hotel Sardonia~ a long loud familiar bellowing could be heard.

HEEE HAW   Heehaw   Heehaw

Everyone knew it was Sardi calling for the little lady and Percy to hurry up. He was always eager to see them.

After their happy greeting, Sardi would eat his dinner. He was a very, very old donkey, yet amazingly healthy and alert. Sardi enjoyed his days. Growing old meant more treats, and always lots of love and attention. Every day was a blessing!

For Percy, he had things to do. His mother knew his schooling would continue. From early on, it had been part of his life. If you own a puppy or dog, it is extremely important that the pet be well mannered. A spoiled and out of control dog can destroy a home and ruin good family relationships. This should never ever be allowed to happen.

Percy and his mother went to classes twice a week at an excellent training club for dogs. Percy had already learned manners and how to get along with other dogs. His next step was learning to heel. This meant walking very close to his mother and following her every footstep.

He also learned to jump and to stand absolutely still while a person touched his back. He learned to sit and to stay down for periods of time. These were all part of the examination he would take, later.
GUESS WHAT?

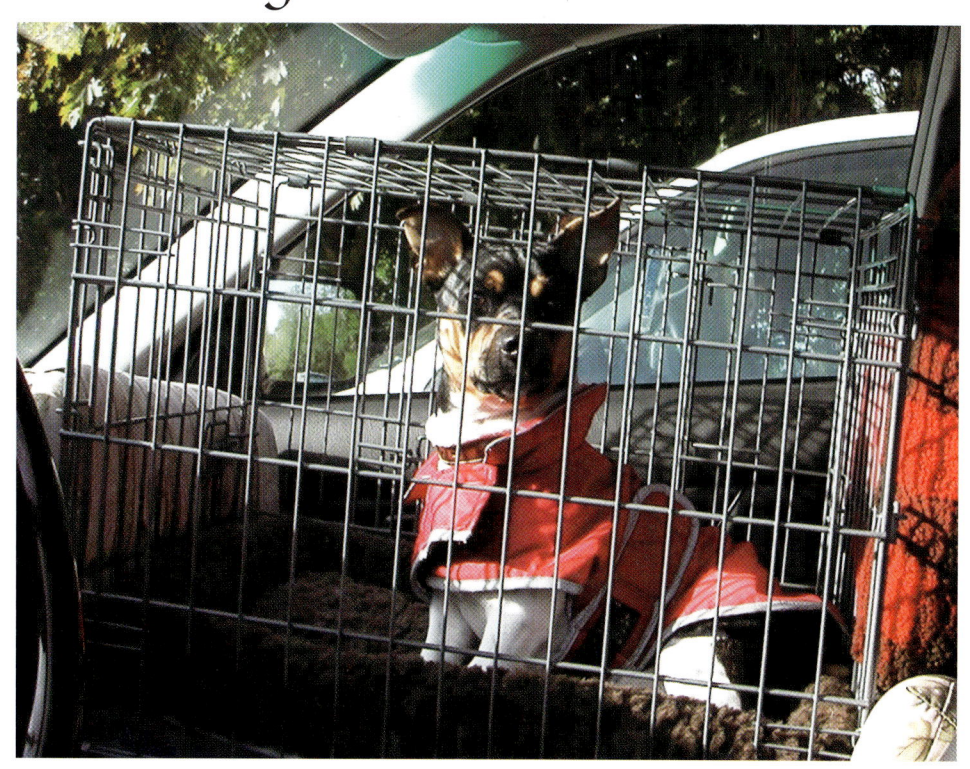

Traveling safely in his dog crate, and looking very handsome in his favorite coat, Percy was taken to a dog show.

After many months of training, and practicing at home, Percy was ready. Arriving at the show, early, on a cold wet and windy morning in May, Percy did not know what to expect. He was excited and

"Oh Dear"

a little nervous. He shivered and looked around. Percy was not very happy.

All the new sights, sounds and smells made him anxious. He wasn't sure about things.

When it was time for Percy and his mother to go into the show ring to take the test, Percy tried to follow his mother and the judge's instructions. But the newness of it all, and his young age with no show experience worked against him.
It did not go well! They failed the test.

Once outside the show ring, Percy heard the kind words of his mother, telling him everything would be all right. She was proud he had gotten this far in his training. Her gentleness, in the face of failure, worked wonders. Instead of being discouraged, Percy kept his spirits up. They would try again in the future.

Afterward, Percy wrote a letter to his brothers at Ramblewood Kennels in South Carolina. It was written, from dog to dog, factual and fun.

Dear Brothers Lance and Arthur,

Well today I wish you had been here to cheer me on with a few good barks. My mother took me to a dog show and we entered our first class. We have been practicing and practicing ever since I can remember. I knew all the commands and I was ready. But wouldn't you know, the day was awful and rainy. A lot of people stayed home. Who would want to walk around in a cold downpour? Well the judge came and so did ten people for our class. Two girls were assigned to help the judge. They were called Stewards. Apparently no adults volunteered, so two cute girls were in the ring with the judge. Let me tell you, they were really sweet in their blue jeans with purple and pink tops and their flip-flops. They were giggling and having fun together. When it came time for Mother and me to do our test, everything was going fine. We did the heel on leash, the figure eight exercise, stand for exam and then it was time for the heel off leash. We were coming down the line, perfectly, heading toward the tent where the girls were sitting, wiggling their feet. The judge said "About Turn". Mother turned, but I didn't. I wasn't paying attention to her. Instead, I ran over to visit the girls. Oops, I shouldn't have done that. The judge said we got a failing score because I didn't obey and she didn't correct me. Mother wasn't mad or upset. She said the girls were really friendly and I would need to learn to ignore cute and tempting when in the show ring.

I will keep you posted. Love you guys,

Your Brother,   Percy

Months later, they went to another show. This time everything went much better.

Percy got a passing score on the test! In fact he earned a blue ribbon. This was called his "first leg" toward a Novice Title.

At the show the next day, they tried again. But there was a problem. Percy started to bark when he entered the ring. Barking was definitely not allowed during the test. Also, he did not watch his mother carefully, and with that, they failed.

Several more months went by and they continued to practice at home and in class. When the pair felt ready, off they went to another show. This time Percy paid good attention and passed the test easily. In fact he got the highest score in the class. His mother and those around him were very proud! He had another blue ribbon and his second leg toward his Novice Title.

Percy's Ribbons

One more passing score was needed to complete the title. They took the test the next day. Percy did all of the exercises with confidence. But at the last minute, when he came flying over the jump in the

'Recall', instead of stopping in front of his mother, he ran right past her and out of the ring. What a big mistake! He failed the test! Obedience was very hard! Even as smart as he was, at times he couldn't keep his mind on what he should be doing. His free spirit just took over.

Being honest, failing to complete the test was disappointing, as they had worked very hard to get it right. But they would not give up. His mother understood this and she was there to help and encourage Percy. (Sometimes things in life and life itself can be very hard. You have to keep your spirits up and keep trying!) Who knew what the future might hold; and having friends would help. Percy had many at school.

Percy's classmates from Youngstown All Breed Training Club

Sweet Pea   Molly   Sadie   Dreamer

Emmitt   Jasper   Sara   Percy   Sage   Rachel

Misty Blue   Gipsy   Silky   Rugby

Cole   Stormy   Lucy   Charlie   Cody

Sundance   Kiyoshi   Mystery   Aura   Casey   and   Hope

Perhaps heavenly support might also help. It was that time of year, in the fall, when a special ceremony was held at their church. It was called The Blessing of Pets.

St. Peter of The Fields, Rootstown, Ohio

Percy was taken to receive a blessing. From the farm across the road, a big red rooster scurried over to the churchyard to see what was going on. "Red Rascal" was a very large bird and he was a bully!

As the people and their pets arrived, the bold rooster strutted about the grounds. He rushed at several of them. Many felt uncomfortable. Percy's mother did not want the rooster to set his sights on Percy. This rooster could be dangerous if he pecked or clawed at Percy. Just like at Percy's first puppy school class, his mother had to scoop him up in her arms to keep him out of harm's way. The priest, Father David, gave the blessing. Percy was blessed, and when the rooster came near, Father David blessed him too with holy water. The spray surprised and startled the rooster. He did not like it! Red Rascal ruffled his feathers, and wisely decided to run back home.

That was a blessing for all.

With the show season over, Percy settled in to life at home where he had lots of places to explore. Fortunately, when he was a puppy, his mother had taught him to come to the sound of a whistle. He could be far away, and when he heard the whistle, he came running, instantly. By obeying this training, it might someday save his life. Dogs can easily run off and get into trouble without thinking about it. By knowing the rule, that the word 'Come' or the sound of the whistle meant Come, Quickly, Instantly, Percy was protected from things he might not expect. Percy was good at getting out of sight. But when he heard the whistle or her call, "COME":

He came, fast as lightening!

Percy would arrive at his mother's feet, pull up to a dead stop and look up with those eager eyes, as if to say, "I heard you, here I am!" He then always got a treat! She kept treats in her pocket, knowing that a reward for good behavior meant success when training. Percy never failed to come when called. Because he minded so well, his mother had peace of mind when they were outside together. With her confidence in him, Percy was given more and more freedom. The little black, white and tan hunting dog, traveling through the woods with his nose to the ground, was a common sight. He was born to hunt and just loved his life in this beautiful country.

Without a doubt, one of Percy's favorite adventures was riding on the tractor. At The Enchanted Cottage there was a large tractor barn, named The Tractor Palace. It was home for several tractors, "High Steppin Sam", "Miss Millie Sawgrass", "Putt Putt" and at times "Big Blue".

The Tractor Palace

Percy got very excited when he saw his mother heading for that building, because High Steppin Sam was Percy's favorite tractor and it was in there. Percy had learned to ride on High Steppin Sam and he was always eager for a trip. His mother had taught him how to get on board. He would climb into her arms and then be lifted way up high, on to the big tractor seat. He would sit there, quietly, until she could climb up and sit beside him. He would then eagerly get on her lap, as she started the tractor and drove it out of the building. Percy thought he was in charge. With his ears standing straight up, he gave his best attention to the ride.

Heading Out

Percy listened to the roar of the engine and felt the throb of power as the tractor growled and lurched along. As it traveled, he could feel the bumps when the tires rolled over uneven surfaces. Sometimes he was jostled back and forth with force but that did not scare him. His mother kept her arms around him. He was always safe.

Since he spent most of his life living so close to the ground, he liked being way up high. On the tractor he felt very tall. And since he could see for a long distance, it was like being on top of the world. He never tired of riding. What youngster wouldn't like to be with him! "Would you take a ride with Percy on High Steppin Sam?"

A Ride In The Meadow

On their rides, Percy and his mother had to trust one another. Percy had to believe he was safe. The loud sounds and strange motion of the tractor would have frightened most dogs. But he knew his mother would take care of him. He trusted her. On her part, she had to trust that Percy would not panic and jump out of her arms and off the tractor. That would have been very dangerous.

Trust is being able to truly count on a person or being, even if it is a dog. When sharing someone's trust, you must honor it and protect it. Trust is very special! Percy and his mother knew, by trusting in each other, they could enjoy many safe and beautiful rides.

The days of driving through the meadow ended as the colorful leaves of fall blew away and a cold north wind arrived. It was December. Outside activities needed a warm jacket and Percy often wore his winter coat. Snowflakes swirled, and the days drew closer and closer to Christmas. For Percy and his family, Christmas was the best time of the year.

Goodness in life was everywhere. There were celebrations of faith, the sharing of gifts, and the pleasures of friendship.

Percy and his mother visited the elderly at a nursing home. They delivered gifts and met new people as they worked to assist their local animal shelters.

It was a happy and busy time for all. Great Grandmother Whiteside's cookies baked in the old oven. Gifts were wrapped. The little lady and her husband could hardly wait for Christmas. The dogs were excited too. They knew something good was about to happen. Finally it was Christmas Eve. As the couple departed for church, Percy and Winston were left at home.

They rested near the fire and kept watch over the stockings that were hung.

On this night there was a beautiful sense of peace, calm and stillness. It was once again silent night, Holy Night.

At home, "not a creature was stirring." Percy made certain of that. He checked regularly, and would never have permitted a mouse to be running around in his house, particularly, at Christmas!

Soon the dogs were fast asleep and the hours slipped by; Santa would be there before morning. He never failed.

Sometime during the night Santa came, and "yes" he left presents!

Once up, Percy and Winston knew exactly what to do. They wanted to open their presents immediately. Eagerly they watched, as each gift was unwrapped. The sound of the crinkling wrapping paper was almost too exciting for words. Then the 'grab it' happened. They had no manners at all. It was just grab and run with the new bone, the tug-of-war toy and other gifts. Their excitement was completely out of control. Percy and Winston raced around the living room, chasing one another with each new toy. Of course there were dog treats and Christmas goodies.

What a wonderful day!

It couldn't get any better!

Percy paused to rest after all the excitement. He had the greatest gift, his family. And they were blessed with his presence in their lives.

He truly was the perfect puppy, and with time he had grown up to be a terrific dog. Best of all, he possessed a heart of gold. Deep in this beautiful heart was true faithfulness to the little lady and her husband. It was a precious bond they all shared.

Percy's delight could be seen in his greeting whenever they returned home, after being away. His little tail would go ninety miles and hour and he would leap for joy on his brilliant little legs. Kisses and wiggles told you, nothing could replace his happiness. He had his family, he had his home and he couldn't wish for more.

While Percy's story of 'Growing Up' recounts some of the events and accomplishments he achieved in his early years. Be assured he continued to have many wonderful adventures throughout his life. He had the good fortune to live in the company of those he loved, in a magical world of joy at The Enchanted Cottage.

He will be long remembered as a 'Teddy' who's sweetness knew no bounds, who's eagerness knew no end and who's loving nature captivated all he met.

THE END

Percy is a merry fellow, keen in all his ways.
He touched our hearts forever, bringing smiles to all our days.

ABOUT HELEN

Long before writing the stories of "Percy", Helen enjoyed a warm heart in the writing of her poetry. From early childhood, she has written on little slips of paper, on sheets from a tablet, on Christmas cards, whatever and whenever her feelings and observations welled up and she paused to record them.

Family and friends have known a little poet lives among them.

The two books about Percy, each subtitled, The Tale of a Teddy Roosevelt Terrier, are Helen's first writings in prose. They were inspired by her love of Percy and her family and her desire to write and photograph their special time and place in her life. She hopes the reader will feel her triumph over sadness, explore the love and rewards of sharing life with man's best friend, and learn some valuable lessons on life, as seen through their adventures. The photographs taken by Helen and Teresa add beautiful, if not magical, reality to the stories.

ABOUT TERESA

Teresa Waldvogel-Otto and her husband Tom were the breeders of Percy. Giving credit where credit is due, Percy and his loving nature, would not have been so wonderful, if they had not imprinted his life at the beginning. Those first days, weeks and months in a dog's life form a foundation that is either, good, bad or in between. With them, the start is always good. Of importance, is Teresa's gentleness, which is felt with an extremely kind and loving touch. When she speaks to her four legged "furkids", her voice has a quality that draws attention, yet has a comforting way. Her dogs listen to her and at the same time know they are very loved. She has a powerful imprint on puppies. Breeders and owners alike respect her, as she is totally sincere, refreshingly honest and genuinely compassionate.

Man or beast is fortunate she walks this earth.

Teresa's biography, found in "PERCY" The Perfect Puppy, reveals a lifetime devoted to dogs. The Teddy Roosevelt Terrier is her chosen breed. For Teresa and her husband Tom, serious work goes into their successful breeding and showing program. Known by the name, Weebits Teddy Roosevelt Terriers, many of their puppies have gone on to achieve recognition as UKC Champions.

Fortunately for all, Teresa's Granddaughter, Hunter, has become an accomplished handler in the show ring. In her free time, she is a welcome help with the Teddies.

Hunter possesses the gentle hands and ways of her grandmother and most assuredly will carry on Teresa's legacy.

Hunter with her dog, Champion Weebits Ghost of PTM

In discussing the breed, a Teddy Roosevelt Terrier must have 'go to ground' hunting instincts, rectangular body profile, muscular build with strong bones, short powerful legs, smooth coat, and natural bob or docked tail. These terriers are very intelligent, energetic, sociable and long lived, and do well in the country or city. With Percy as proof, they are extremely devoted to their families. Here are some fine examples of puppies, photographed by Teresa, from one of their litters.

Splash PENNY MOON

Moose RAVEN

These little ones show their sturdy long bodies, short legs, and good solid bones, characteristic of quality Teddy Roosevelt Terriers. Who can resist those wide-eyed, beautiful faces?

Copper BUDDY

Sire of the puppies, CH Weebits Gamblin Man of CCK, "Casino"

Their dam, CH Weebits Against All Odds, "Gin Gin"

And lucky for our family, one of their puppies has joined his forever family with Helen's daughter Sara, son-in-law Jimmy and their twins, Audrey and William.

Beautiful "Copper"

Acknowledgements

With the publication of "PERCY" The Perfect Puppy, Helen had no plans for a second book. Copies flew from coast to coast and even overseas. Feedback from children and adults was favorable, with many being touched by the story of a saddened heart finding joy in a new puppy. Books were placed in libraries and schools and in the hands of dog lovers, and given to charities and organizations for fund raising.

One day, Helen received an email from her friend, Sharon Phillips. In this email, Sharon relayed a question asked by her young friend who had received the book. Ashley asked, "Is the Enchanted Cottage real"? Helen wrote back "Yes it was." Helen started thinking about the innocence and sincerity of the question. It reminded her of the question posed by "Virginia" asking if Santa Claus were real. Both young ladies wanted to know if someone and something, having a magical or enchanted being, were real. The answer is "Yes". In the hearts of man, Santa Claus truly lives, and in the hearts of those who love dogs, The Enchanted Cottage truly exists. They are real.

Touched by Ashley's question and further reached by other suggestions that Helen might consider writing more about Percy, Helen wrote the true tale of his 'Growing Up'. For the young and the tender hearted who love dogs, this is a love story. For all who have been a part of it, we warmly say "thank you".

Ashley and "Triscuit"

Above is pictured Ashley and Sharon's dog, Triscuit. Adorned with wings, Triscuit is a Parson Terrier, playing the part of a fairy. Lori Baker took the photograph at the Youngstown All Breed Training Club in Austintown, Ohio. Permissions were happily given to include this photograph.

Helen needed assistance in obtaining photographs of Percy riding on the tractor. Helen asked her good friend and naturalist Ethan Kistler, to help. Ethan followed High Steppin Sam and the pair, through the meadow, taking the delightful pictures of this adventure. Ethan was at home in the meadow.

Pictured below is Ferrier, Brian Hoover, with Sardi. We are grateful to Brian for trimming Sardi's hooves for over a decade. For certain, Brian's skillful work and loyalty to his charge have added many, many years to Sardi's life.

Finally, words become inadequate for thanking our husbands, Larry White and Tom Otto. Without their love and support, life would be empty. The sharing of ideas, the combining of talents and the pleasure in one's company makes life wonderful. Both men are great animal lovers. Very often either can be found with a dog or dogs on the lap, assisting in any number of ways with their care. Home is where the puppies get spoiled and our men are Chief Spoilers.

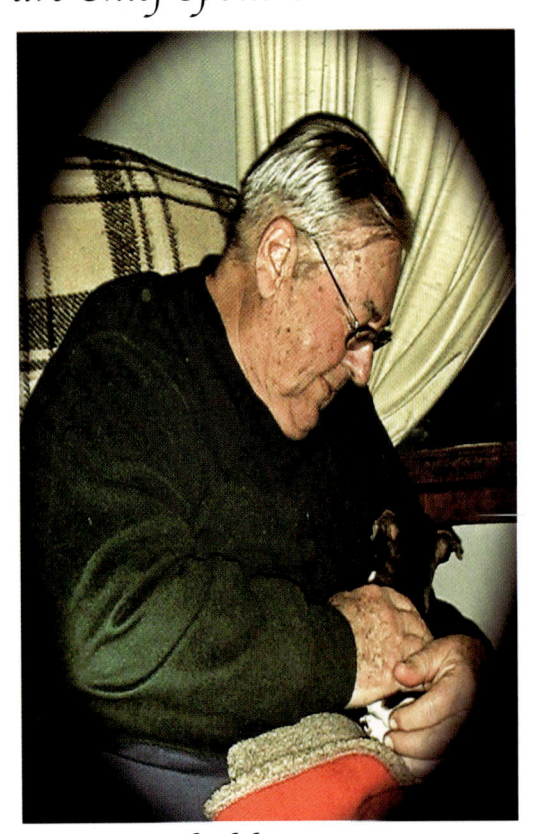

Larry holding Copper　　　Tom with Percy's mother Flame

We end our tale on a happy 'note of Faith'!

* God Bless *